THE
UNDERTAKER

BY ADAM STONE

BELLWETHER MEDIA · MINNEAPOLIS, MN

jB
Undertaker
WITHDRAWN

Are you ready to take it to the extreme?
Torque books thrust you into the action-packed world
of sports, vehicles, mystery, and adventure. These books
may include dirt, smoke, fire, and dangerous stunts.
WARNING : read at your own risk.

Library of Congress Cataloging-in-Publication Data

Stone, Adam.
  The Undertaker / by Adam Stone.
     p. cm. -- (Torque: pro wrestling champions)
  Includes bibliographical references and index.
  Summary: "Engaging images accompany information about the Undertaker. The combination of
high-interest subject matter and light text is intended for students in grades 3 through 7"--Provided by
publisher.
  ISBN 978-1-60014-640-4 (hardcover : alk. paper)
  1. Undertaker, 1965---Juvenile literature. 2. Wrestling--United States--Biography--Juvenile literature. I.
Title.
  GV1196.U54S78 2012
  796.812092--dc22   2011012517

This edition first published in 2012 by Bellwether Media, Inc.

Printed in the United States of America, North Mankato, MN.

CONTENTS

At WrestleMania 26, more than 70,000 fans were on their feet. The **main event** was about to begin. The Undertaker was putting his undefeated record on the line against Shawn Michaels. He had won his last 17 WrestleMania matches.

Fans cheered as the match began. The Undertaker immediately forced Michaels into a corner and took control of the fight. He tried to put Michaels away with a **chokeslam**, but Michaels escaped.

QUICK HIT!

"Undertaker" is a term for a funeral home director. The Undertaker sometimes forces his opponent into a casket next to the ring!

SHAWN
MICHAELS

Wrestling Name: _ _ _ _ _ _ _ _ _ _ The Undertaker

Real Name: _ _ _ _ _ _ _ _ Mark William Calaway

Height: _ _ _ _ _ _ _ 6 feet, 10 inches (2.1 meters)

Weight: _ _ _ _ _ _ _ 299 pounds (136 kilograms)

Started Wrestling: _ _ _ _ _ _ _ _ _ _ _ _ _ _ _ 1984

Finishing Move: _ _ _ _ _ _ _ Tombstone Piledriver

The men battled inside and outside the ring. Michaels went for a pin, but The Undertaker **kicked out** just in time. He hurled Michaels to the mat with a powerful chokeslam. Then he delivered a crushing **Tombstone Piledriver**. Michaels got up, and The Undertaker performed another one. Then he covered Michaels for the pin. He had extended his WrestleMania winning streak to 18 matches in a row!

WHO IS THE UNDERTAKER?

The Undertaker was born on March 24, 1965 in Houston, Texas. His real name is Mark William Calaway. He is the youngest of five brothers. Calaway was a good basketball player in high school. Many of his coaches thought he could be a professional player.

After high school, Calaway went to Angelina College in Lufkin, Texas. He played basketball there for two years. Then he moved to Texas Wesleyan University (TWU).

Calaway was also training to become a wrestler. His basketball coaches tried to talk him out of it. However, Calaway knew what he wanted. He left TWU after one year. He was ready to wrestle.

11

QUICK HIT!

Calaway won his first title in 1989. He defeated Jerry "The King" Lawler for the USWA Heavyweight Championship.

JERRY
"THE KING"
LAWLER

Calaway started out in small wrestling leagues. His first wrestling name was Texas Red. In 1989, he signed with the United States Wrestling Association (USWA). He wrestled as The Master of Pain and The Punisher.

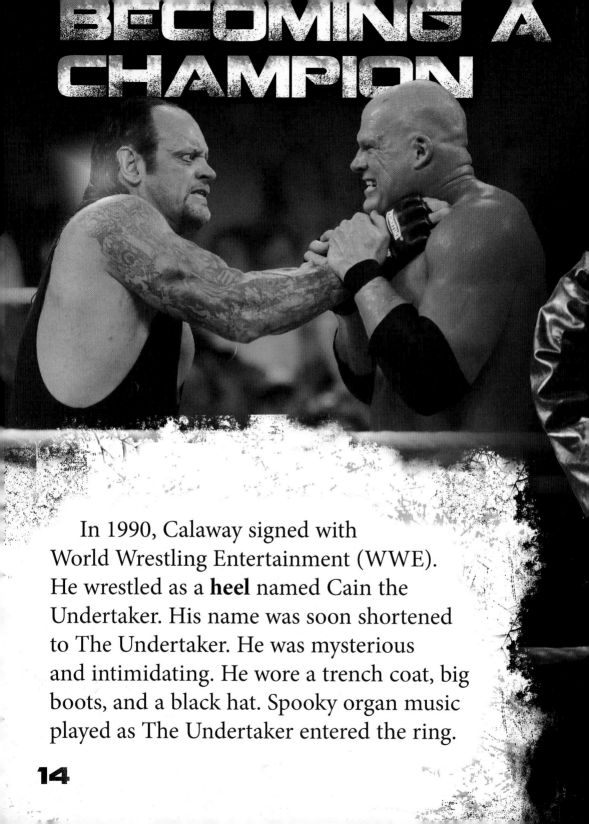

In 1990, Calaway signed with World Wrestling Entertainment (WWE). He wrestled as a **heel** named Cain the Undertaker. His name was soon shortened to The Undertaker. He was mysterious and intimidating. He wore a trench coat, big boots, and a black hat. Spooky organ music played as The Undertaker entered the ring.

QUICK HIT!

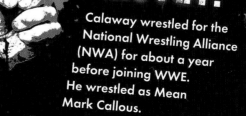

Calaway wrestled for the National Wrestling Alliance (NWA) for about a year before joining WWE. He wrestled as Mean Mark Callous.

QUICK HIT!

Before a match begins, The Undertaker looks at his opponent and rolls his eyes back into his head.

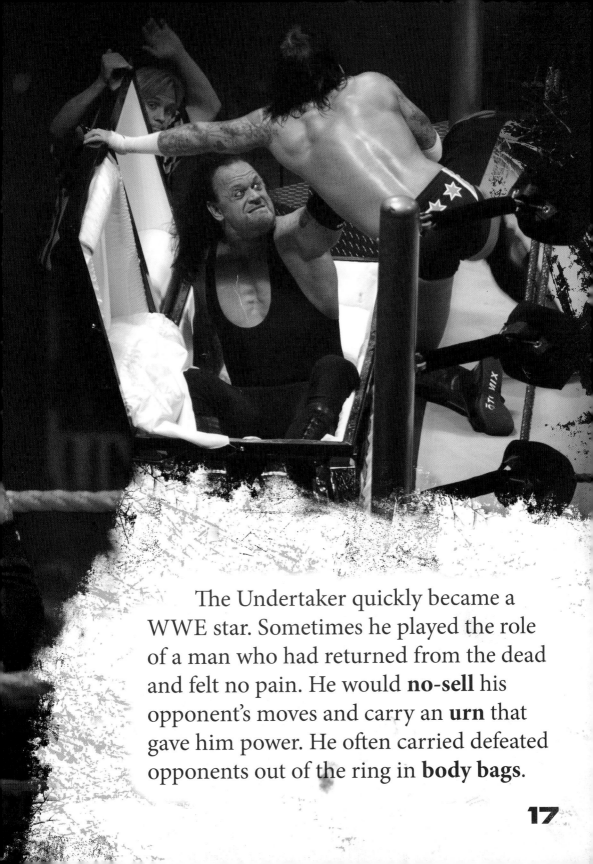

The Undertaker quickly became a WWE star. Sometimes he played the role of a man who had returned from the dead and felt no pain. He would **no-sell** his opponent's moves and carry an **urn** that gave him power. He often carried defeated opponents out of the ring in **body bags**.

BIG BOOT

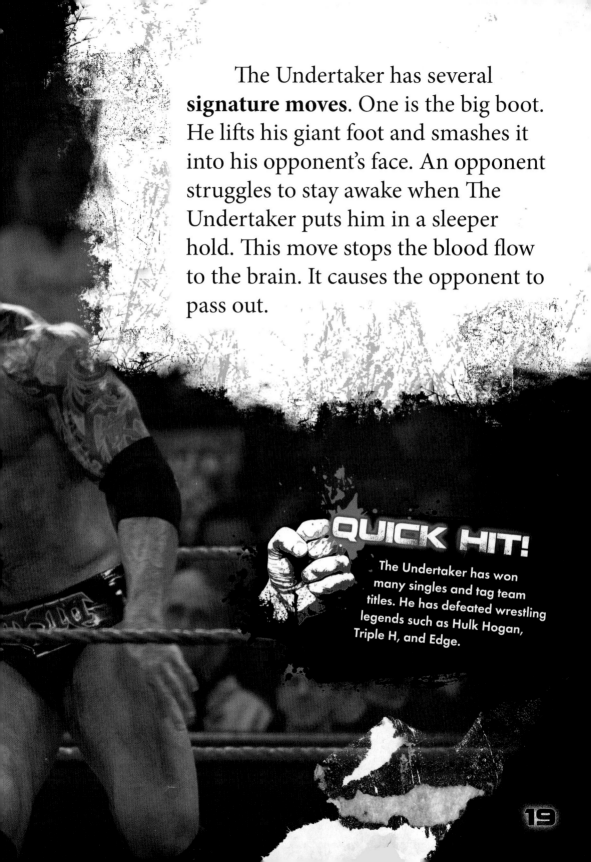

The Undertaker has several **signature moves**. One is the big boot. He lifts his giant foot and smashes it into his opponent's face. An opponent struggles to stay awake when The Undertaker puts him in a sleeper hold. This move stops the blood flow to the brain. It causes the opponent to pass out.

QUICK HIT!

The Undertaker has won many singles and tag team titles. He has defeated wrestling legends such as Hulk Hogan, Triple H, and Edge.

The Undertaker's Tombstone
Piledriver is one of the most merciless
finishing moves in WWE. He holds his
opponent upside down. Then he falls
to his knees, driving the opponent's
head into the mat. The move is so
powerful that the opponent is usually
knocked out. The Undertaker's cold,
unfeeling nature makes him a threat
to all who face him in the ring.

GLOSSARY

body bags—large bags used to hold dead bodies

chokeslam—a move in which a wrestler picks up his opponent by the throat and slams him down to the mat

finishing moves—wrestling moves meant to finish off an opponent so that he can be pinned

heel—a wrestler seen by fans as a villain

kicked out—escaped a pin

main event—the most important match at a wrestling show; the main event is the last match of the show.

no-sell—to not react to an opponent's moves

signature moves—moves a wrestler is famous for performing

Tombstone Piledriver—one of The Undertaker's finishing moves; he picks up his opponent, holds him upside down between his knees, and drops him headfirst onto the mat.

urn—a container that holds the ashes of a dead body

TO LEARN MORE

AT THE LIBRARY

Black, Jake. *The Ultimate Guide to WWE*. New York, N.Y.: Grosset & Dunlap, 2010.

O'Shei, Tim. *Undertaker*. Mankato, Minn.: Capstone Press, 2010.

Sullivan, Kevin. *Undertaker*. New York, N.Y.: DK Publishing, 2009.

ON THE WEB

Learning more about The Undertaker is as easy as 1, 2, 3.

1. Go to www.factsurfer.com.

2. Enter "The Undertaker" into the search box.

3. Click the "Surf" button and you will see a list of related Web sites.

With factsurfer.com, finding more information

INDEX

The images in this book are reproduced through the courtesy of: David Seto, front cover, pp. 9, 15, 18-19, 20-21; Wire Image / Getty Images, pp. 4-5, 6, 8, 13; MCT via Getty Images, pp. 10-11; Getty Images, pp. 12-13; Picture Perfect / Rex USA, p. 14; John Smolek, p. 16; Vishal Somaiya / Alamy, p. 17.